We like to swing.

1

We like to whizz and spin.

We like to yell in tunnels.

We like to splish, splash and splosh.

5

We like to run in the sun and dig in the sand.

We like to squelch in the mud and stamp on the twigs.

We like to jump off a log and
hit a stump with a stick.

We like to hop like frogs

and spring like squirrels.

And when we get home...

we like to flop.